Who I Am In Christ

Guided Prayer and Scripture Meditation to
Help You Discover and Step Into Your True
Identity In Christ

By Sandra J. Christiansen

DEDICATION

This book is dedicated to my amazing parents (lovingly called Mommy & "Dad Baby"), who raised me in the Christian faith. Even when I fell away and went through my rebellious and questioning phases, they were always behind the scenes praying for me. They provided abundant love and a firm foundation for me to grow on and flourish. I am overwhelmingly grateful that God placed me in their care. This book would not be possible without them.

TABLE OF CONENTS

INTRODUCTION 1

CHAPTER 1: YOUR IDENTITY 9

CHAPTER 2: HOW TO USE THIS BOOK............................13

CHAPTER 3: DAY 1 - I AM A CHILD OF GOD.....................19

CHAPTER 4: DAY 1 PRAYER AND SCRIPTURE MEDITATION 23

CHAPTER 5: DAY 2 - I AM LOVED.....................................29

CHAPTER 6: DAY 2 PRAYER AND SCRIPTURE MEDITATION 33

CHAPTER 7: DAY 3 - I AM FORGIVEN 39

CHAPTER 8: DAY 3 PRAYER AND SCRIPTURE MEDITATION 45

CHAPTER 9: DAY 4 - I AM VALUABLE 51

CHAPTER 10: DAY 4 PRAYER AND SCRIPTURE MEDITATION 55

CHAPTER 11: DAY 5 - I AM SET FREE 61

CHAPTER 12: DAY 5 PRAYER AND SCRIPTURE MEDITATION 65

CHAPTER 13: DAY 6 - I AM A NEW CREATION 71

CHAPTER 14: DAY 6 PRAYER AND SCRIPTURE MEDITATION 77

CHAPTER 15: CONCLUSION 83

REFERENCES 85

INTRODUCTION

Welcome to *Who I Am in Christ*. I want you to know that I've been praying for you. Yes, you. I've been asking God to deliver this book into the hands of each person who He wants to have it. So, if you think that you just happened to stumble upon this book or if a friend recommended it to you, it's no coincidence. God wanted you to have this and to hear the loving message He wants to share with you. I pray that this book will bless you and that you'll be filled with a new excitement for life and a boldness to forge ahead in your true identity.

Before we begin, I feel that it's essential to start with the basics. If you're at a stage where you're exploring Christianity or if you're unsure if you've truly accepted Christ, I want to start by outlining, in plain terms, what that means and how you can move into that relationship. To get there requires a small history lesson first. But it's a thrilling story. So, sit back and enjoy.

God created us and everything in the universe. For that reason, He has authority over us and all creation. He also created angels. One of them, who was the highest and most beautiful of all angels, Satan, did not want to be God's right-hand man (or right-hand angel). Satan wanted to be the one in charge. He didn't want to serve God; he wanted to be the one to be served. Because his pride was out of control, he was cast out of heaven. On his way out, he also led a rebellion of angels that followed him.

God perfectly created us and our world. He also gave us free will to choose what actions we want to take while we're on this earth. So, soon after the first people were created, the head of the rebellion came to mess with them. Satan tempted them (first Eve, and then later Adam) into doubting God's goodness and love for them. God had given Adam and Eve a perfect paradise and He had only one rule for them: not to eat of the fruit of that one tree. Although there was only one rule, Eve chose to break it. Since Eve bit into that piece of fruit, things have never been the same. You might ask, "What's the big deal about eating a piece of fruit?" Well, it wasn't really about the fruit.

It was because Eve made a free-will choice to follow a path that promised greatness. Satan lied and told her that the fruit would make her God-like and led her to believe that God was holding something back from her. When she took that bite, she agreed with the lie that Satan told her.

That one action caused chaos in all of God's creation. From that day, we inherited sin and guilt from Adam and Eve. When this happened, God's children were separated from Him because of sin. In our modern-day world, "sin" is usually thought of as simply being an immoral act. But the Bible defines it differently. Romans 14:23 (NIV) says, "everything that does not come from faith is sin." In other words, anything outside of God's plan is sin. It's a dividing line that can't be crossed. So, God set up the world's greatest rescue plan to get us back!

God gave us the ten commandments. He already knew that, in our brokenness and weakness, we would never be able to keep them perfectly. You might ask, "Well, then why bother? Are they just there to make us feel guilty?" The answer is an emphatic no. The law was established because God knew that when we step outside of the boundaries of His commandments, we will suffer consequences, and He doesn't want His children to suffer. The law was also given to us to help us come to the conclusion that we could never be "good enough" to overcome sin on our own. We need a savior to help. Romans 3:20 (NIV) says: "Therefore no one will be declared righteous in God's sight by the works of the law; rather, through the law we become conscious of our sin."

In the Bible, sin is expressed as being a debt. It is a debt that must be paid. So, if you hear someone say that Jesus "paid the price" or "paid my debt," that is what they are referring to.

No one is exempt. Think of the best person that you know. They still fall short of the glory of God. Billy Graham? He fell short. Mother Theresa? She was a sinner as well. We all need saving. Romans 3:23-24 (NIV) tells us: "For all have sinned and fall short of the glory of God, and all are justified freely by His grace through the redemption that came by Christ Jesus."

A perfect sacrifice was required to pay this debt. It couldn't be paid by just anyone. Jesus, who is perfect and flawless, is literally the only one who could pay the debt. Jesus took our place. Instead of us having to pay the penalty ourselves, He took on the sins of the world and died as our substitute. You might ask, "Why doesn't God just forgive us? Why did there have to be a sacrifice?" Hebrews 9:22 (NIV) tells us: "In fact, the law requires that nearly everything be cleansed with blood, and without the shedding of blood, there is no forgiveness."

God is a holy and righteous judge. He couldn't simply let the debt go unpaid. Thankfully He's not only just, but He is also loving. In His love, He made a way for our debt to be paid.

These days, many people believe that there are multiple ways to be reconciled to God. But God, the creator of the universe, disagrees. If there were any other way to pay this debt, that would mean that Jesus died for no reason. That is why God lovingly tells us that Jesus is the only way, so there will be no question.

When Jesus was crucified, the debt was paid in full, once and for all. Not only was Jesus crucified, but He rose from the dead. He actually defeated death! Because of this, the curse that separated us from God was broken. We can now be one with God again. Although we won't truly see Him face to face until we're in heaven, we get to experience His kingdom here on earth through a relationship with God and with others.

God offers everyone the free gift of this "paid debt." All you have to do is agree with Him and accept the gift. Some people think that you have to "clean yourself up" before you can come to God. But that is absolutely false. There is nothing that we can do to clean ourselves up. God has to do that for us.

Sadly, many people who call themselves Christians become the self-proclaimed "moral police" over others. The truth is that we all need help. Even the moral police. Will we become perfect immediately after becoming a Christian? No. But God sees the heart, and that is what He cares about. We strive to do our best because of what Christ has done for us. He knows we'll mess up. But He knew that from the beginning - and He still chose you and me.

The main steps to accepting Jesus are:

1. Acknowledge that you are a sinner and that you need God's help.

2. Believe that Jesus died for your sins and rose again. If you need help with this, ask Him to help you believe.

3. Ask Him to become your Lord and Savior. In other words, you're asking Him to become the leader of your life from now on and the forgiver of your sins.

4. Tell Him that you accept His gift of salvation.

Once you accept this gift, nothing can ever separate you from God. Again, God sees inside hearts. If you sincerely ask (and don't merely go through the motions because you feel pressure to), God has you covered!

I want to assure you that there is no wrong way to do this. There aren't specific words that make it the "correct" way. This can all be done from the heart, in a frank, honest conversation with God.

Before we go on with the rest of the book, I feel it's important to cover one more subject. Because all of our sins: past, present, and future have all been forgiven, we might ask if our actions matter. Yes, they do.

First, because we are loved by God, we are called to spread that love to others, and secondly (again), God knows what is in each of our hearts. Paul even addresses this question in the Bible. In Romans 6:1-2 (MSG), he says: "So what do we do? Keep on sinning so God can keep on forgiving? I should hope not! If we've left the country where sin is sovereign, how can we still live in our old house there? Or didn't you realize we packed up and left there for good?"

Many people think being a Christian simply means acting morally and going to church regularly. They believe if you can sweep all your junk under the rug and pretend everything is ok, then you're in! Even if someone is interested in God's message, they might think, "I could never keep up the good act that long! So why bother trying?"

Honestly, it is understandable why many people have this view. Sadly, it's the way that many Christians have presented themselves for a long time. Since this "cleaned-up-act" is not sustainable long term, we are also sometimes viewed as being hypocrites. Often (sadly), this is correct. Dictionary.com defines hypocrisy as "a pretense of having a virtuous character, moral or religious beliefs or principles, etc., that one does not really possess." We are all sinners in need of help. That is why we need Jesus: because we can't do it on our own. Christians who humbly follow Jesus are genuinely changed over time. But, *only* by God's grace. *Not by our own doing*.

Christianity is not merely a behavior modification program. It doesn't matter if you stay away from bad language, drinking alcohol, the "wrong type" of movies, etc. if you haven't actually accepted God's gift. I'll say it again: God sees inside the heart. Once we've been saved, we start living out of the thankfulness we have to God for saving us. That won't require behavior modification. It will naturally flow from who you are and the new creation that God is making you into. Instead of pretending we're on moral high ground as compared to others, let's get out there and love people and show them that they are loved by God as well.

I hope this helps answer some questions that you might have had. If you are new to Christianity, I would highly encourage you to get connected to a local Christian church in your area. Just as there are no perfect people, there are also no perfect churches - because they are all made up of imperfect people. But we need to lean on each other in this life. None of us can do it alone. We need to come together and build each other up so we can spread God's love to the rest of the world.

I hope this book blesses you and that God speaks to you powerfully through the time you spend with Him.

CHAPTER 1: YOUR IDENTITY

What exactly is identity?

Is it your name?
Your job title?
Your nationality?
Your marital status?
What you've achieved?
The mistakes you've made?
The way you view yourself?
The way that others view you?

The answers to each of these are simply descriptors, actions, or opinions (which are subjective). But, none of them can fully describe the essence of a person or their true identity.

The Oxford Dictionary definition of identity is: "The fact of being who or what a person or thing is."

Would we dare tell an artist that we know more about his sculpture than he does? Or would we tell an inventor that we are better acquainted with the purpose of her creation than she is? We have no problem understanding these earthly concepts. But the same holds true with us (God's artistic creation) and God (our Creator).

Who could ever say who a person is and what their purpose is better than the Creator himself? It doesn't matter what anyone else says about you (including yourself). He still has the final say.

If I say to myself and others, "I'm a tree! I'm a tree!" - it doesn't make me a tree. We might giggle at the thought of that, but we do it every day when we put ourselves down or when we agree with negative comments and opinions that others have about us.

Don't get me wrong; I know that it's challenging to live in this world and keep God's perspective. We're immersed in so many negative messages all day, every day. Yes, there is beauty and good in the world, but our minds tend to latch onto the negative messages unless we actively combat and reject them. That's why taking time to pray and meditate on scripture regularly is so incredibly important. It's to remind us of who we really are.

Why Does It Matter?

You might be asking: "Why does it matter how I view myself?" What you believe about your identity and how you view yourself shapes your entire life. You might not think it has that much of an effect one way or the other, but it literally determines how you approach life and informs every decision you make. That can be life-changing.

If you find your identity in what others say about you, you'll always be chasing the approval of others. If you find your identity in what you accomplish, eventually you'll find that it will never be enough. You'll be on a hamster wheel that you can't get off. If you find your identity in the mistakes that you've made, you'll never feel "good enough." If you find your identity in being a victim of horrible acts committed against you, you will either grow bitter over time or see yourself as not being "worthy." There are many other examples, but you get the picture. The bottom line is this: all of the wasted time and energy you're pouring into pleasing others, trying to accomplish more, or being angry at someone who wronged you, is time and energy that you are taking away from your true purpose. You're being distracted by Satan, our enemy. And it's an easy bait to run after.

You already have everything you need to accomplish God's plans for you in this life. You won't necessarily have everything that *you* want or everything you need to accomplish what *someone else* wants you to do. That's because you don't need those things to achieve your real purpose. Instead of continually striving and wearing yourself out trying to be something that you're not (like a tree!), you can rest in the fact that God has a beautiful plan for you and that

He'll lead you to where He wants you to go (and will also provide you with what you need along the way). When you come to that place of freedom, it will be a massive weight off your shoulders.

CHAPTER 2: HOW TO USE THIS BOOK

My primary purpose in writing this book is to help equip others to not only learn about their true identity in Christ but also how to step into it and live it out.

Because these facts about God and our identity are so counter-cultural, we need to take time and meditate on them regularly. Like anything else we want to get better at, it takes repeated practice. It's not something we can read one time and think, "I'm good! I've got it!". It's something that we need to take in over and over until it sinks in. Even then, we need to remind ourselves continuously. That's why I suggest that this book be used as a practice tool, rather than merely a one-time read.

Not only do we need to practice reminding ourselves of the truth, but we also need to practice rejecting the lies that we hear. We are in a spiritual battle. If you've never heard that before, it means that Satan is still working against us. Jesus already won the war for us. When He was crucified and rose again, He defeated Satan and death, once and for all. Since Satan knows that he can't hurt God himself (because he's not powerful enough), he goes after God's kids. That's us. But there is nothing to fear because God is protecting us. Satan just wants us to *think* that that we have something to fear. That is why it's so important not to agree with him. If he can get us bitter enough, or depressed enough, or angry enough, we can easily lose sight of the uniquely suited purpose that God has for each of us. This is the reason it's so vital to reject his lies.

Lies we hear (from others, from Satan and even from ourselves) usually have a kernel of truth at the center. That's because those lies are easiest to believe. But that doesn't mean they are the truth. Any twist of the truth is still a lie. It's dangerous to agree with and internalize those lies, because it will affect the way that you see yourself, and subsequently, how you approach life and your purpose. During the prayer and scripture meditation portion, we will be asking God to help us recognize and reject the lies that come our way, and replace them with His truth.

There are six sections of this book. Each section is designed to be a short, 10-minute read/meditation. My recommendation is to read one section a day, six days of the week (taking a break one day a week for the Sabbath). The more you read and internalize God's truth, the better equipped you'll be to walk in your true identity. The sections are as follows:

Day 1: I Am A Child of God
Day 2: I Am Loved
Day 3: I Am Forgiven

Day 4: I Am Valuable

Day 5: I Am Set Free

Day 6: I Am A New Creation

Each section has a short introduction and then prayer and scripture meditation that follows. After you've read the introduction for a specific day, you can always skip right to the daily meditation and prayer in the future if you prefer.

To receive a free printable pdf of flashcards featuring all of the Bible verses covered in this book, please visit: **sandrajc.com/identity**. Instructions on how to download them will be delivered to your inbox!

Prayer and Scripture Meditation

Meditation simply means to deeply focus on something for a certain period of time. So, as you read, focus on each of the words and what they mean to you. All of the language in the prayers and personalized scripture is spoken from the

first-person point of view. I purposely wrote it in this way so that, as you read, you can internalize the words as being personal to you.

I chose scripture from different versions of The Bible (see Copyright page for more information). Each of the verses were hand-picked. I chose a version for each passage that would be easily understood in today's modern language.

Here's what you can expect in the Prayer and Meditation section for each day.

1. First, I suggest that you find a time of day and place where you can be quiet and not distracted. I understand this isn't always possible. We lead crazy and busy lives. But, when you can, take a few minutes out of your day to give God time to speak directly to your heart. When we're fueled with His words, we're able to approach the day, armed with His truth.

2. The Prayer section of each day is based on the A.C.T.S. Method of Christian Prayer. This method is based on the Lord's Prayer, which is how Jesus taught us how to pray. It is expressed as the acronym: A.C.T.S. Here is what each of the letters stands for:

- Adoration: Give God honor and praise for who He is. He is Lord over all and the only one who is truly worthy of our praise.

- Confession: Honestly confess your sins to God and tell Him what you're struggling with. There's no need to fear! He already knows everything about you, and He still loves you.

- Thanksgiving: Let Him know what you're thankful for. Even if you're going through the toughest time of your life, there are still people, things, and situations to be grateful for.

- Supplication: Pray for the needs of others and yourself.

3. The scripture meditation portion of each day is not designed to simply read through quickly. To combat the negative messages and lies we're continuously fed, we need to not only read, but also internalize God's truth about ourselves. One tool to help us do this is to verbalize the truth aloud. Speaking words aloud helps to secure them into our long-term memory. Studies show that when we add an active measure to learning (such as speaking aloud or writing), the words become more distinct in long-term memory. Let's do all we can do to make God's truth stick! My suggestion is to read and meditate on the scripture and then say it aloud twice. After each of the scripture passages, I change the language to make it personal. So you'll be reading (and then verbalizing) the verse as a statement that is true about you (sometimes it will be God speaking directly to you).

My pastor regularly reminds us that faith is believing that God is who He says He is and that He'll do what He says He's going to do. I've always loved that simple explanation. When we put our faith in a specific *outcome*, we set ourselves up for disappointment. But, if we put our faith in the fact that God *will* do what He says He's going to do (and not put our faith in just getting the outcome we desire), it is a much healthier and accurate view of God and of faith. So, let's grow our faith together and immerse ourselves into who God says we are.

CHAPTER 3: DAY 1 - I AM A CHILD OF GOD

You are a child of God. Yes, *you*.

Take a moment to let that sink in fully. The almighty creator of the universe is *your father*.

Do you believe that statement? Maybe you've heard this a few times over the years, and it just seems silly to you, or simply something nice-sounding that Christians say. Or you might have had a strained relationship with your earthly father, so the concept doesn't translate in your mind. Or, perhaps you believe that it's true, but you struggle to keep that perspective from day to day.

If any of these describe you, you're not alone. It's completely understandable. We are so immersed in our world, that it's hard to take off our "world glasses" and see things from another perspective: God's perspective.

But here's the good news: no matter how you *feel* about it, *it is still the truth*!

This holds true with earthly parents as well. Your biological parents will always be your parents. It doesn't matter if you no longer have a relationship with them. It doesn't matter if you have amazing adoptive parents who you consider your real parents. It doesn't even matter if you've been emancipated or have never met them, they will always be your parents. Nothing can change that fact.

The same thing holds true for God. He is your heavenly dad regardless if you think you're not "good enough" to approach Him, or even if you flat out deny Him. God literally formed you in your mom's womb (Psalm 139:13). He also lives outside of time, meaning that He knows every action that you'll take throughout your lifetime, and He still chose to create you. He still loves you. He even thinks you're worth dying for! Once you accept the invitation into His family, nothing can separate you from God (refer to the introduction if you'd like more information on accepting this invitation). So, when fears or insecurities creep in, remind yourself that nothing can stop Him from being your father. It's not a variable. It's just who He is.

Relationships can be complicated, to say the least. If you've had a strained or broken relationship with a parent, it can be devastating. But in God's family, He is the perfect, loving father who loves you in a perfect way. It can be hard to let this sink in if you've had a difficult (or no) relationship with your earthly father. That is completely understandable. I pray, right now, as I write these words, that God will heal your heart and transform what thoughts and feelings come to your mind when you think of God as your father.

You are a child of God. You are literally a princess or a prince in His Kingdom! Have you ever thought of it that way? You are a precious child of God, and nothing can change that fact.

In early 2019, after having a DNA test, a Maryland man discovered that he was actually an African prince. This led to a 5000-mile journey to meet his family. At the airport, he was met by hundreds of people. He said: "People were just clapping, chanting, cheering. It was an unbelievable moment. When we got in front of the palace, I just sat there for a moment. Just like, wow. This is too much to take in."

We might feel exactly like this man did when he discovered that he was of a royal bloodline. It can be "too much to take in." But God beckons us to step into our true identity. Our child-of-God identity. He doesn't want His precious children choosing to live in slavery while He is offering us freedom and His kingdom.

Often times, it's not that we don't want to accept the Kingdom, it's that we feel unworthy of it or "not good enough" to hold the title. It could also be that we feel unsure if we're ready to accept the responsibility that comes along with holding the Princess or Prince title. The fantastic news is that God has already equipped us with everything we need to fulfill our unique role in His family. You're not lacking anything.

When we believe we're missing something, whether it be specific gifting, status, beauty, etc., it's because we're listening to the wrong voices. Instead, God assures us that we already have everything we need inside of us. Plus, He will provide help from others and extra tools that we need along the way as we follow His path. So, you don't have to wait for a future when you are ten pounds lighter, or more successful, or more educated, or [fill in the blank]. You can start living God's purpose for you today. You are a child of God. He loves His kids. He desires to help us and lead us. We need to believe the truth about Him and ourselves - and then take action.

What is "action" in this case? God doesn't make us His kids just so we can name-drop or sit back and enjoy the good life. He always wants us to share our good life and love with others.

Now, let's move on to some prayer and scripture that will help instill this into our hearts and minds.

CHAPTER 4: DAY 1 PRAYER AND SCRIPTURE MEDITATION

Opening Prayer

Father, I adore you. My heart leaps for joy that You chose me as your child and that You are my Heavenly Father!

Many times I act like a rebellious teenager and do what I want to do. I long to be obedient to you, Father. But then I run the other way. I'm so sorry for that. I am exceedingly grateful that you are always there waiting with open arms, no matter what.

Living in this world and constantly ingesting so many negative messages has left me weary. In my head, I know that you are my Father and I am your child. But many times my heart forgets. Please help me to truly hear and fully internalize your words.

Write the following scriptures on my heart and never let me forget them. Let your words give me strength to step into my true identity as your child and reject any messages that say otherwise.

In Jesus' holy name, break the power over any lies that I am believing about you as my Father. Bring them to my mind and then let your truth take their place. Amen.

Scripture Meditation

Read each of the following scripture passages, as well as the personalized version of each one, several times. Then say each one aloud, at least twice. Let the words wash over you. Instead of rushing through the reading, take time to internalize and own each passage.

2 Corinthians 6:18 (NIV)

I will be a Father to you, and you will be my sons and daughters, says the Lord Almighty.

Now, let's make that verse personal. Imagine God speaking this over you:

"I will be a Father to you, and you will be my child, says the Lord Almighty."

John 1:12 (NRSV)

But to all who received him, who believed in his name, he gave power to become children of God.

Now, let's make that verse personal.

"I have received God and I believe in His name. So, He gave me the power to become His child."

Galatians 3:26 (WEB)

For you are all children of God, through faith in Christ Jesus.

Personalized version:

"I am a child of God, through faith in Christ Jesus."

1 John 3:1a (NIV)

See what great love the Father has lavished on us, that we should be called children of God! And that is what we are!

Personalized version:

"What great love the Father has lavished on me, that I should be called a child of God! And that is what I am!"

Ephesians 1:5 (NASB)

He predestined us to adoption as sons through Jesus Christ to Himself, according to the kind intention of His will.

Personalized version:

"He predestined me for adoption as His child through Jesus Christ, according to the kind intention of His will."

Romans 8:16 (NIV)

The Spirit himself testifies with our spirit that we are God's children.

Personalized version:

"The Spirit himself testifies with my spirit that I am God's child."

Ephesians 2:19 (NIV)

You are no longer foreigners and strangers, but fellow citizens with God's people and also members of His household.

Personalized version:

"I am no longer a foreigner or a stranger, but a fellow citizen with God's people and a member of His household."

Romans 8:14&15b (NASB)

All who are being led by the Spirit of God, these are sons of God... you have received a spirit of adoption as sons by which we cry out, Abba! Father!

Personalized version:

"I am being led by the Spirit of God, so I am a child of God... I have received a spirit of adoption as His child and I cry out, Daddy! Father."

Closing Prayer

Father, thank you for the gift of your word. I am so thankful that I am your child, and a sibling to Jesus and the rest of your family! What a privilege and honor. Help these words sink into my heart and soul. Let them sink deeper in, every time I read and speak them. Please guide me through this day and let the knowledge that I am your child frame every thought I have and also dictate every action I take.

Thank you for walking along side of me every moment of the day. You are truly a loving Father! In Jesus' name. Amen.

Day 1 Exercise

Is there anything else that you want to talk to your heavenly Father about? Sometimes people or situations will pop into your mind. If nothing immediately comes to your mind, take a moment to quiet your mind and heart. Ask the Holy Spirit to bring to mind anything that God might want to talk to you about. Be still for a few more moments and then end your time with Him today by sharing a Father and child heart-to-heart conversation.

CHAPTER 5: DAY 2 - I AM LOVED

God loves you. Not a future, cleaned-up version of you. But, you. Just the way you are. There is nothing that you can do to make God love you more than He already does. There is also nothing you can do that will make Him love you any less. Isn't that freeing? You don't have to run after God's love and strive to be a "better person" so that He'll love you. He already does. He's never in a bad mood and will never change His mind about you. His love is unconditional and never-ending.

Even if we say that we have unconditional love for another person or pet, in actuality, we don't. If your kids are having a melt-down or the dog poops inside the house, the love meter might go down a half a point. Although I'm saying that tongue-in-cheek, the truth is, we don't have the capacity to love unconditionally. The concept of pure unconditional love is foreign to us.

The Bible tells us: "God is love. Whoever lives in love lives in God and God in them." 1 John 4:16b (NIV)

Did you catch that? God *is* love. He isn't just loving (although He is), and He doesn't just give love (although He does), but He actually *is* love. It is His character. It is the essence of who He is.

If you've struggled with feeling loved in your life, I understand entirely. I've never been married. So, for countless years, I carried the belief that something was wrong with me. I felt unloved and unlovable.

Then I did what we all do. I gathered evidence to support my "case". Every time I had feelings for a man that weren't reciprocated, I would tell myself, "See! This just proves that I'm unlovable!" I wouldn't say those exact words, but they were the feelings and emotions that I held onto. Whenever we want to find "evidence" that we aren't loved, we will always find it - and the enemy will be there to lend a helping hand.

By God's grace, I now know and wholeheartedly believe the truth. I am loved, and I am lovable, regardless of how anyone on earth feels about me. I'm not going to lie; it's been a long journey to this place. But God is good and faithful. I'm so thankful that I'm on the other side.

Similarly, if we feel unworthy of love, we tend to push away or reject the love that comes our way. If you can identify with this feeling, the amazing news is that it is just that: a feeling. Feelings are not truth. Feelings are only indicators of where your heart and head are. The danger lies in interpreting feelings as facts. The longer you hold onto them, the more time they have to marinate inside. Just like I held onto the feelings that I was unloved and unlovable (that over time turned into beliefs), these feelings and fake evidence must be destroyed once and for all - and replaced by the truth of God's love. If we don't take this action, we will end up living under a false identity. Don't get me wrong. God does the heavy lifting here. This is not something that we can do on our own. But we have to agree with the truth and choose to reject the lies. This is not an easy task. Especially if we've believed these lies for a long time. But it will get easier with time and practice. God will help you every step of the way. One way that He does this is through the gift of the Holy Spirit.

When you accept Christ as Lord and Savior (as the forgiver of your sins and the leader of your life), you're immediately forgiven, and you are also given His Spirit. This means that God's Spirit actually comes to live inside of you. The Spirit is there to help you along the way. John tells us: "The Helper, the Holy Spirit, whom the Father will send in My name, He will teach you all things, and bring to your remembrance all that I said to you." John 14:26 (NASB) He is always there to direct you, help you remember the truth, and combat the lies.

If you are feeling unloved, unlovable, or unworthy of love, take heart! I believe that God brought this book to you for a reason. I pray that you will hear His love note loud and clear and that you will fully accept His everlasting, unconditional love for you.

Lastly, what is the purpose of God wanting us to know and believe that we are loved? Is it just so that we can feel warm and fuzzy inside? No. It's that He wants us to *spread it to others*! Just as we have been loved, we should love others. We are God's representatives in this world. We are called to carry His kingdom, His message, and His love to others.

Let's move to some scripture meditation and prayer to help us internalize these facts.

CHAPTER 6: DAY 2 PRAYER AND SCRIPTURE MEDITATION

Opening Prayer

God, you *are* love! How incredible to ponder that fact. You are not only loving, but you actually *are* the very essence of love! Without you, no one would ever experience love.

Many times I push your love away or chase after fake love instead of your true love. I'm so sorry for that. I am incredibly thankful that you are always faithful to me, even when I am not faithful to you.

I'm tired of striving to find love in other places. Why would I bother going anywhere else than the source of all love? Compared to what I'm used to, your perfect love is hard to wrap my mind around. And sometimes I question why you would love me in the first place. Please continue to remind me that You love me, eternally and unconditionally. Help me to remember that Your love has nothing to do with who I am or what I do. It's all about who You are: Love.

Write these scriptures on my heart and never let me forget them. Let your words give me the strength to step into my true identity as your beloved child and reject any messages that say otherwise.

In Jesus' name, break the power over any lies that I'm believing regarding love and your love for me. Replace them in my mind with your truth. Amen.

Scripture Meditation

Read each of the following scripture passages, as well as the personalized version of each one, several times. Then say each one aloud, at least twice. Let the words wash over you. Instead of rushing through the reading, take time to internalize and own each passage.

Jeremiah 31:3b (NRSV)

I have loved you with an everlasting love; therefore I have continued my faithfulness to you.

Now, make that verse personal. Imagine God speaking this over you: "I love you with an everlasting love. Therefore, I will continue my faithfulness to you."

1 John 4:16a (NIV)

And so we know and rely on the love God has for us.

Now, the personalized version:

"I know and rely on the love God has for me."

1 John 4:16b (NIV)

God is love. Whoever lives in love lives in God, and God
in them.

Personalized version:

"God is love. I live in love, so I live in God and God lives
in me."

John 15:13 (NASB)

Greater love has no one than this, that one lay down his life for his
friends.

Personalized version:

"Greater love has no one than this, that Jesus laid down His life for
me!"

John 3:16 (MSG)

This is how much God loved the world: He gave his Son, his one and only Son. And this is why: so that no one need be destroyed; by believing in Him, anyone can have a whole and lasting life.

Personalized version:

"This is how much God loves me! He gave his Son, his one and only Son. And this is why: so that I won't be destroyed. By believing in Him, I can have a whole and lasting life."

1 John 4:19 (NASB)

We love, because He first loved us.

Personalized version:

"I love others because God first loved me."

1 John 3:16 (NIV)

This is how we know what love is: Jesus Christ laid down his life for us. And we ought to lay down our lives for our brothers and sisters.

Personalized version:

"This is how I know what love is. Jesus Christ laid down His life for me! And so I lay down my life for others."

Note: If this verse seems a little scary, it simply means that you will spend your life loving and helping others.

Romans 8:38-39 (NIV)

For I am convinced that neither death nor life, neither angels nor demons, neither the present nor the future, nor any powers, neither height nor depth, nor anything else in all creation, will be able to separate us from the love of God that is in Christ Jesus our Lord.

Now, make this verse personal. We'll simplify this one a bit:
"I am convinced that there is absolutely nothing that can separate me from the love of God that is in Christ Jesus,

my Lord."

Closing Prayer

Father, thank you for loving me. I am so thankful that I don't have to do anything to gain your love. Thank you for the reassurance that there is nothing, no one, and no circumstance that could ever separate me from you. Please help these scriptures sink into my heart and soul. Let them sink deeper in, every time I read and speak them. Please guide me through this day and let the knowledge that I am eternally and unconditionally loved by you frame every thought I have and dictate every action I take. In Jesus' name. Amen.

Day 2 Exercise

Take a few minutes to sit quietly with God. Meditate on the fact that you are loved eternally and unconditionally. Tell Him personally what that means to you. He is always there to listen when you need Him.

CHAPTER 7: DAY 3 - I AM FORGIVEN

You are forgiven.

What feelings or emotions does that sentence conjure up inside of you? Relief? Thankfulness? Uneasiness (because you don't think you deserve it)? Confusion (because you're not sure why you need to be forgiven)?

First, if this stirs up feelings of confusion, I urge you to read the introduction to this book. If you're feeling relief or thankfulness, those are valid and healthy responses. If you're feeling uneasy or you believe that you're not worthy of forgiveness, I'm thrilled that you're reading this right now.

If you're feeling unworthy of forgiveness, that's because it's true. That's right. We are not worthy. We could never do anything to make ourselves worthy. The Apostle Paul reminds us: "For it is by grace you have been saved, through faith—and this is not from yourselves, it is the gift of God - not by works, so that no one can boast." Ephesians 2:8-9 (NIV)

Forgiveness is a free gift from God. We didn't do anything to deserve it, and we never could. Paul makes it clear that forgiveness is not gained by works, because otherwise, we would want to take the credit.

If you've accepted God's invitation to be a part of His family, then you are forgiven. It doesn't matter if you *feel* like you're forgiven. Remember, feelings are simply indicators of where your heart and head are. They are not facts. So, regardless of how you feel about it, you are forgiven.

God lives outside of time. This means that He knew you before you were born. He knew every action you'd take, every decision you'd make, every mistake you'd make - and He still chose you. He still chose to create you. He loves you, and you are forgiven *no matter what*.

Plus, He doesn't just do a little "dusting job" on us. He doesn't even do a deep clean on us. He literally makes it as if our sin never existed in the first place. God says: "I, even I, am He who blots out your transgressions, for my own sake, and remembers your sins no more." Isaiah 43:25 (NIV)

God doesn't hold grudges. He doesn't wait for a fight to bring up our wrongdoings of the past like humans do. Instead, He blots them out.

God does require us to come to Him to acknowledge and confess our sins. He also requires us to repent (which simply means to turn around) from our sins. John tells us: "If we claim to be without sin, we deceive ourselves, and the truth is not in us. If we confess our sins, He is faithful and just and will forgive us our sins and purify us from all unrighteousness. If we claim we have not sinned, we make Him out to be a liar, and His word is not in us." 1 John 1:8-10 (NIV)

Paul tells us in Romans 8:1 (NIV): "Therefore, there is now no condemnation for those who are in Christ Jesus." So, if you have confessed a sin and have turned from it, and you're still carrying guilt over it, that is not God's voice. Satan knows how to push our buttons. So, if he knows we feel guilty about something, he will continue to bring it back to our minds. Use the power that God has given you and fight against this. The way to combat lies is with God's truth. You might even say aloud something along the lines of: "I've confessed this sin to God and have turned from it. I know that I'm forgiven because of Jesus' sacrifice. There is no condemnation for me because I am in Christ Jesus."

Although I covered this in the introduction, I believe it bears repeating. Because all of our sins have been forgiven, we might think that is a license to do whatever we want to.

Why not just go crazy? Paul addresses this question in Romans 6:1-2 (MSG). He says: "So what do we do? Keep on sinning so God can keep on forgiving? I should hope not! If we've left the country where sin is sovereign, how can we still live in our old house there? Or didn't you realize we packed up and left there for good?"

Once we've been saved, we start living out of the thankfulness we have to God for saving us. That won't require behavior modification. It will naturally flow from who you are and the new creation that God is making you into. This does not mean that all temptation disappears. It can actually mean the opposite. Satan doesn't want you to realize your real identity, so he'll push back. But we have no reason to fear. God wants to help us live out who we really are, and He'll help us every step of the way.

Lastly, God not only wants us to *know* that we are forgiven - He forgives also to show us a perfect example. Because we are forgiven, we are also called to forgive others. In some cases, this can be extremely difficult. But we are called to follow His example.

If you think this is impossible, God will help you. Even if your head and heart don't agree, when you take this step of obedience to forgive, God will honor it. You can talk to Him like you're talking to a friend. Simply say (something along the lines of), "God, I don't know how to forgive this person, and frankly, I don't want to. But I want to be obedient to your command to forgive. Please help me." Then simply say the words (even if you don't "feel it"): "Father, through the power of Jesus Christ, I forgive [person's name] just as you have forgiven me." You might need to repeat this over an extended amount of time. But God knows your heart, and He understands. Just keep letting it go until it's completely gone.

Even if you think (or know) that the person doesn't "deserve" forgiveness, don't continue to carry this burden. It's only going to destroy *you*. And remember, we don't deserve God's forgiveness, yet He still gives it to us. He is calling us to do the same.

Because of Jesus, that person or people no longer have power over you. Don't pick the burden up after Jesus has relieved you of it. I can guarantee that Satan will be there to remind you of what they did to you. Just continue to say, "Father, through the power of Jesus Christ, I forgive [person's name] just as you have forgiven me." Continue to do this until you have peace. It will come. It might take time. But it's not a race. God will help you and guide you.

Now let's move on to the prayer and meditation for today.

CHAPTER 8: DAY 3 PRAYER AND SCRIPTURE MEDITATION

Opening Prayer

God, you are my redeemer! Without you, I would be stuck in my sin and doomed to an eternal penalty that I could never pay. In your love, you reached down and saved me. Jesus, I praise you that you are the only one worthy and able to pay the price for me - and you did!

There are times when I am prideful and think, "I don't need to be forgiven! I'm not *that* bad!" Other times, I feel like there's no way I can approach you because what I've done is too horrible to be forgiven. I confess that I am wrong either way. I am so thankful that you have forgiven me! I know you do this not because I deserve it, but because of your amazing, unconditional love for me as your child.

I'm tired of being stuck in sin! I know it's holding me back from being the real me. God, right now, I confess the sin that I am stuck in. [Take a moment with God to confess any sin that you are currently feeling unable to move on from]. Please help me to turn away from my sin and then move forward, free of this burden.

I'm also tired of carrying guilty feelings over my past. I know you forgive me, but sometimes I don't feel worthy of your forgiveness, so I willingly pick that guilt back up. Right now, I lay it down at your feet. Remind me that there is no condemnation for those in Christ. Free me from this burden, so I can live the life that you want me to live.

I come before you with an overflowing and thankful heart. I know that I don't deserve to be forgiven, but in your love, you choose to forgive me anyway. What an amazingly generous gift! In the hardest times, please remind me that in the same way that you forgave me when I didn't deserve it, that I should also offer grace and forgiveness to those who have wronged me.

In Jesus' holy name, break the power over any lies that I'm believing regarding forgiveness. Replace them in my mind with your truth. Amen.

Scripture Meditation

Read each of the following scripture passages, as well as the personalized version of each one, several times. Then say each one aloud, at least twice. Let the words wash over you. Instead of rushing through the reading, take time to internalize and own each passage.

Isaiah 43:25 (NASB)

I, even I, am the one who wipes out your transgressions for My own sake, and I will not remember your sins.

This beautiful verse is already personalized! Imagine God speaking directly to you.
"I, even I, am the one who wipes out your transgressions for My own sake, and I will not remember your sins."

Hebrews 8:12 (NRSV)

For I will be merciful toward their iniquities, and I will remember their sins no more.

Let's personalize this verse. Imagine God speaking to you.
"For I will be merciful toward your iniquities, and I will remember your sins no more."

1 Corinthians 6:11b (NIV)

You were washed, you were sanctified, you were justified in the name of the Lord Jesus Christ and by the Spirit of our God.

Personalized version:

"I am washed, I am sanctified, I am justified in the name of the Lord Jesus Christ and by the Spirit of my God!"

2 Corinthians 5:17-19 (MSG)

Anyone united with the Messiah gets a fresh start, is created new. The old life is gone; a new life burgeons! Look at it! All this comes from the God who settled the relationship between us and Him, and then called us to settle our relationships with each other. God put the world square with himself through the Messiah, giving the world a fresh start by offering forgiveness of sins. God has given us the task of telling everyone what He is doing.

We'll personalize this scripture and simplify it a bit.
"I am united with the Messiah, so I have a fresh start! I'm created new. My old life is gone, and a new one is emerging!"

1 John 1:9 (NIV)

If we confess our sins, He is faithful and just and will forgive us our sins and purify us from all unrighteousness.

Personalized version:

"When I confess my sins, God, who is faithful and just, will forgive me my sins and purify me from all unrighteousness."

Ephesians 1:4 (NASB)

He chose us in Him before the foundation of the world, that we would be holy and blameless before Him.

Personalized version:

"He chose me in Him before the foundation of the world, that I would be holy and blameless before Him!"

Psalm 103:10-12 (NIV)

He does not treat us as our sins deserve or repay us according to our iniquities. For as high as the heavens are above the earth, so great is his love for those who fear Him; as far as the east is from the west, so far has He removed our transgressions from us.

We'll personalize this scripture and simplify it a bit as well.
"As far as the east is from the west, so far has He removed my transgressions from me!"

Closing Prayer

Father, thank you for your forgiveness. I am so thankful that when I had no way to pay my debt, you paid it on my behalf. Thank you for the reassurance that there is no condemnation for those who are in Christ! Once I have confessed a sin to you and have turned from it, I don't need to continue to carry that burden.

Please help these scriptures sink into my heart and soul. Let them sink deeper in, every time I read and speak them. Please guide me through this day and let the knowledge that I am forgiven frame every thought I have and dictate every action I take. In Jesus' name. Amen.

Day 3 Exercise

If you feel stuck in sin or guilt or if you're having a hard time forgiving someone, take some time out with God and talk it through with Him. He doesn't want you to stay stuck there. He wants to help you out of that place. It might take some time, but God is a patient and loving Father. Let Him help you bear your burden.

CHAPTER 9: DAY 4 - I AM VALUABLE

You are extremely valuable!

In fact, God thinks that you are worth dying for. Literally. This is another concept that is hard to wrap our brains around. The majority of our population regularly feels like they are "not good enough." Where does this incorrect belief come from? And why is it so pervasive?

Similar to the way that we tend to feel unloved or unlovable, through our experiences in life, we tend to internalize the message that we're not good enough in some way or another. This is no coincidence.

From a human point of view, we might say that it is because of the messages that we've received throughout life. It's a compilation of all the perceived "failures" in our lives. Imagine two sisters who receive very different messages from an early age. One might be doted on by their parents and others because they are "so cute and adorable." Although it might be unintentional, the other sister receives the message loud and clear that she doesn't measure up in that area. On the other hand, the "cute" sister might not do as well in sports or academics as the other sister. So, she ends up feeling inadequate as well - just in a different area of life.

We need to remind ourselves that no one can be successful in every area of life. Each of us is equipped with exactly what we need to be successful in the plans that God has for us. But, most of us fight against this. We're unhappy and sometimes resentful that we aren't equipped in the same way that someone else is.

There's a quote that I've always loved, which is attributed to Albert Einstein. Although there is controversy over if he is the one who truly said it, it is brilliant none-the-less. The quote is: *"Everybody is a genius. But if you judge a fish by its ability to climb a tree, it will live its whole life believing that it is stupid."*

That is precisely what we do to ourselves when we try to live out someone else's life or purpose! If you're not sure of your purpose, God will help you find it. Keep in mind that in our culture, many times, we think of a "purpose" as one big, giant thing that we have to discover. That might be the case, but most likely not. You don't need to look for one big "thing to do" and wonder why you can't find it. Instead, through small acts of obedience to God, He can lead you through your life and to your purpose. Instead of just one big thing, it more likely is many seemingly "smaller" things. Most times, God doesn't give us the whole picture. He wants us to take these small steps of obedience, even when they don't make sense from a human perspective. That is what a journey of faith is all about.

From a spiritual point of view, when we focus on being like everyone else and then wonder why we don't feel "good enough," Satan takes these insecurities and runs with them. He won't miss an opportunity to remind you that you "don't live up" in a specific area. This can lead to feeling useless and worthless. That is exactly where he wants each one of us. If we feel useless and worthless, we won't take action to find our purpose or take those steps of obedience. We settle into a "why even bother trying?" mentality.

This can be disguised if we're successful in another area. Maybe God is nudging you to do something that, to the rest of the world, seems crazy. What if an accomplished surgeon was being nudged by God to quit his job and create art? Most people would think that was absolutely nuts. He might say to himself, "I don't even really know anything about the art world. It only makes sense to stay where I'm at."

Don't get me wrong. I'm not telling everyone to go out and quit their job. This is just an example. But, what if the surgeon knew that healthcare wasn't his passion from the beginning? What if it was his parents' dream for him and not his? This can lead back to the "why bother trying?" attitude, just on the opposite end of the spectrum.

This is why it's so important to internalize that you are extremely valuable - just the way you are. The value of anything is the price someone is willing to pay for it. God sent His perfect son, Jesus, to pay the price for your sins and mine (if there's any confusion on this, please refer to the introduction to this book). That means that, in God's eyes, you are literally worth dying for. Not a movie-version of a man telling the woman he loves that he would die for her... but an actual sacrifice to free you from bondage.

You are priceless. God says it, and He is the only one who has a say regarding who we truly are. No one else has that authority. Don't let others define you. Their opinions simply don't matter. I know believing that is easier said than done. But the longer you practice meditating on your true identity in Christ, over time, it will become easier to believe and internalize. Who He says you are outweighs anyone else's opinion of you - including your own.

Let's move to some prayer and scripture meditation.

CHAPTER 10: DAY 4 PRAYER AND SCRIPTURE MEDITATION

Opening Prayer

God, you are so creative! When I think of everything that you've created, I am in such awe! Most of the time I take it for granted. But, when I take time to really study a flower, the sky, water or a bird, I stand in amazement! And the human body? Wow! Just thinking of every intricate detail and how you make everything work together is simply awe-inspiring. On top of it all, you didn't create our bodies to merely be machines. You breathed life into every one of us and hand-crafted each individual personality and set of gifts!

Most of the time I don't view my body through your eyes. Instead, I focus on everything that I dislike about it. I get so hyper-focused on all of the things that I wish I could change about my body, that I forget what an amazing gift it has been. I do the same thing with my personality and gifts. I find myself longing to have what others have, instead of being grateful for what I've been given.

I also spend a lot of time feeling insecure and not good enough. When this happens, I dwell on negative thoughts about myself and internalize destructive messages from others. Sometimes the messages from others are intentional and sometimes I interpret them in the wrong way. Either way, I still carry them with me.

I confess all of this to you, God. I'm so sorry that I've been viewing your beautiful creation in such a dishonorable way. Help me to shed these negative views about myself, my body and my worth and remind me of who I really am.

I am so thankful that you created me just the way I am! I am grateful that my worth isn't dictated by other's opinions of me or even my opinion of myself. Instead you have proven to me, through Jesus' death, that you think I am priceless - and you're the only one who gets a say in the matter.

Please replace all of my wrong thinking with your truth about me. Write these scriptures on my heart and never let me forget them. Let your words give me the strength to step into my true identity as your child and reject any messages that say otherwise. In Jesus' name, break the power over any lies that I'm believing regarding my worth. Replace them in my mind with your truth. Amen.

Scripture Meditation

Read each of the following scripture passages, as well as the personalized version of each one, several times. Then say each one aloud, at least twice. Let the words wash over you. Instead of rushing through the reading, take time to internalize and own each passage.

Genesis 1:27 (NASB)

God created man in His own image, in the image of God He created him; male and female He created them.

Now make this verse personal.

"God created me in His own image!"

Ephesians 2:10 (NIV)

For we are God's handiwork, created in Christ Jesus to do good works, which God prepared in advance for us to do.

Personalized version:

"I am God's handiwork, created in Christ Jesus to do good works, which God prepared in advance for me to do!"

Proverbs 31:10 (MSG)

A good woman is hard to find, and worth far more than diamonds.

Personalized version:

"I am worth far more than all the diamonds in the world!"

Romans 5:8 (NIV)

But God demonstrates his own love for us in this: While we were still sinners, Christ died for us.

Personalized version:

"God demonstrated His love for me in this: While I was still a sinner, Christ died for me."

1 Peter 2:9 (NIV)

But you are a chosen people, a royal priesthood, a holy nation, God's special possession, that you may declare the praises of Him who called you out of darkness into his wonderful light.

Personalized version:

"I am chosen. I am part of a royal priesthood, a holy nation. I am God's special possession. I will declare the praises of Him who called me out of darkness and into His wonderful light!"

Psalm 139:14 (MSG)

You shaped me first inside, then out; you formed me in my mother's womb. I thank you, High God—you're breathtaking! Body and soul, I am marvelously made! I worship in adoration—what a creation!

Because this verse is already personalized, say it aloud again.

In **Isaiah 43:4 (MSG)** God says:

That's how much you mean to me! That's how much I love you! I'd sell off the whole world to get you back, trade the creation just for you.

Imagine God speaking those words over you. Say it aloud and let it sink into your heart.

1 Corinthians 6:20 (WEB)

You were bought with a price. Therefore glorify God in your body and in your spirit, which are God's.

Personalized version:

"I was bought with a price. So, I will glorify God in my body and in my spirit, because they belong to God."

Closing Prayer

Father, thank you for creating me! You did an amazing job! In the times when I start to feel worthless, help me to see myself through your eyes. When you look at me, you see a precious and treasured child who is worth more than all the diamonds in the world! Replace my negative thoughts with this beautiful picture.

Please help these scriptures sink into my heart and soul. Let them sink deeper in, every time I read and speak them. Please guide me through this day and let the knowledge that I am a priceless treasure frame every thought I have and dictate every action I take. In Jesus' name. Amen.

Day 4 Exercise

If you are struggling with believing that you are truly valuable, set some time aside to have a talk with God. Tell Him why you have such a hard time believing it. Then ask Him to help you to replace your reasons with His truth.

CHAPTER 11: DAY 5 - I AM SET FREE

You have been set free!

You may ask: *"From what?"*

Because of Jesus' death and resurrection, you are not only free from the penalty of sin, but you are also free from what seemingly threatens to crush us in this life. Satan wants us to believe that he still has power over us, but because of Jesus' sacrifice, he has no power. We don't have to listen to his lies and accusations. Through God's power, we have the ability to resist him. James 4:7 (NASB) tells us: "Submit therefore to God. Resist the devil, and he will flee from you."

We can tell him, "No! I was bought at a price, and I belong to Jesus Christ."

Satan wants us to forget that we're free and willingly walk into a prison. You might ask: "Who would do such a thing?" And yet, we do it all the time. It usually starts small. Sin always looks appealing! If it didn't, we would never be tempted. But once we take that shiny bait, similar to a fish being caught, we let him reel us in. Once we're caught, it can seem impossible to get away. The longer we stay in sin, the harder it can seem to escape from it.

Believe me, these tailor-made false prisons seem 100% real. If they didn't appear real, we wouldn't continue to fall for the bait.

Virtual reality headsets and games are becoming more popular as the years go on. If you've ever tried one of the newer models, it's almost alarming how realistic they seem. In one of the games, you walk out on a plank high atop of a sky-scraper. Before playing the game, I thought to myself, "This is silly. I'll obviously *know* in my head that I'm in my living room!" Boy, was I wrong! The amazing power of sight and sound made it feel like I was on that plank, high above the city streets below. I couldn't believe how real it felt and sounded.

After my first VR experience, I immediately thought to myself, "This is exactly what Satan does to us! Our fears are the same as a virtual reality plank. It's all just an illusion." But boy, does it *seem* real. Satan puts his version of VR goggles on us and leads us to believe that we're on a scary plank high above the city, just about to fall off - when, in reality, we're safe and sound in God's "living room." We need God's tools and the Holy Spirit to help us decipher when we have Satan's VR goggles on.

God not only unlocked the cell and let us out of jail, but He actually destroyed the entire jailhouse! So, when we set up our own cardboard box prison and willingly let ourselves be locked up by Satan, it grieves God's heart.

Paul puts it perfectly when he says: "Christ has set us free to live a free life. So take your stand! Never again let anyone put a harness of slavery on you. I am emphatic about this. The moment any one of you submits to circumcision or any other rule- keeping system, at that same moment, Christ's hard-won gift of freedom is squandered." Galatians 5:1-2 (MSG)

Although Paul mentions circumcision, that is not the main point of this passage. He's saying that since we've been freed, we shouldn't willingly become prisoners, otherwise, as Paul puts it, "Christ's hard-won gift of freedom is squandered."

Don't get me wrong; stepping out of a personal prison is *hard*. Especially if we've lived there for a long time. But He loves us too much to let us *stay* there. He knows how hard it is. But He won't leave us hanging. Our step of faith must be to confess our sin to God, repent from it, and move forward. It might seem impossible. But God specializes in what seems impossible by human standards! If He can create the entire universe, He can certainly help you with your personalized prison.

In Galatians, Paul tells us: "It is absolutely clear that God has called you to a free life. Just make sure that you don't use this freedom as an excuse to do whatever you want to do and destroy your freedom. Rather, use your freedom to serve one another in love; that's how freedom grows. For everything we know about God's Word is summed up in a single sentence: Love others as you love yourself." Galatians 5:13-14 (MSG)

Do you see a theme yet? For every attribute of our identity, God wants us to 1) hear it, 2) accept and believe it as our identity, and then 3) in response, serve and love others out of our identity.

Let's move into today's prayer and scripture meditation.

CHAPTER 12: DAY 5 PRAYER AND SCRIPTURE MEDITATION

Opening Prayer

Jesus, you are my Savior! Because of you, I am absolutely free from the penalty of sin and I'm also liberated to live a life of freedom on earth as well. Wow. I can't even wrap my mind around that. You are such an amazing, loving Savior!

Although I know that I'm free, many times I don't live as though I am. I take on burdens that you're not asking me to carry and other times I willingly step into a prison and allow the enemy to lock me up. I confess this to you, God. I'm so sorry that I've been acting as though I'm still a prisoner after you've paid the ultimate price to set me free.

I am so thankful for the gift of freedom that you've given me. What a blessing! I come to you with a grateful heart, knowing that I am free in this life and also free to live with you for eternity.

Please replace all of my wrong thinking with your truth about my freedom. Write these scriptures on my heart and never let me forget them. Let your words give me the strength to step into my true identity as your child and reject any messages that say otherwise.

In Jesus' name, break the power over any lies that I'm believing regarding my freedom. Replace them in my mind with your truth. Amen.

Scripture Meditation

Read each of the following scripture passages, as well as the personalized version of each one, several times. Then say each one aloud, at least twice. Let the words wash over you. Instead of rushing through the reading, take time to internalize and own each passage.

Romans 6:14 (NIV)

For sin shall no longer be your master, because you are not under the law, but under grace.

Now, the personalized version:
"Sin shall no longer be my master, because I am not under the law, I am under God's grace."

John 8:31-32 (NASB)

So Jesus was saying to those Jews who had believed Him, "If you continue in My word, then you are truly disciples of Mine; and you will know the truth, and the truth will make you free."

Note: According to John 14:6, Jesus is the way, the truth and the life. When we walk through life with Jesus as our leader, we truly get to know Him - and He sets us free!

Let's make that verse personal:
"Because I am a follower of Jesus, I have come to know Him personally - and He sets me free!"

Galatians 5:1 (MSG)

Christ has set us free to live a free life. So take your stand! Never again let anyone put a harness of slavery on you.

Personalized version:

"Christ has set me free to live a free life. So, I will take my stand!! I will never let anyone put a harness of slavery on me."

2 Corinthians 3:17 (NIV)

Now the Lord is the Spirit, and where the Spirit of the Lord is, there is freedom.

Personalized version:
"Now the Lord is the Spirit, and where the Spirit of the Lord is, there is freedom - and the Spirit lives inside of me!"

Jeremiah 23:4 (NASB)

"I will also raise up shepherds over them and they will tend them; and they will not be afraid any longer, nor be terrified, nor will any be missing," declares the Lord.

God is speaking about you in this verse. Read it again and let the words wash over you. Imagine overhearing God speaking about you. You will no longer be afraid or terrified because you have been freed from fear.

John 8:36 (NIV)

So if the Son sets you free, you will be free indeed.

Personalized version:
"The Son set me free, so I am free indeed!"

Romans 8:1 (WEB)

There is therefore now no condemnation to those who are in Christ Jesus, who don't walk according to the flesh, but according to the Spirit.

The personalized version:

"There is no condemnation for me because I am in Christ Jesus. I no longer walk according to the flesh, but according to the Spirit. I have been freed from condemnation!"

Now that we've been set free, what should our response be? In **Romans 6:15-18 (MSG)**, Paul tells us what true freedom is:

So, since we're out from under the old tyranny, does that mean we can live any old way we want? Since we're free in the freedom of God, can we do anything that comes to mind? Hardly. You know well enough from your own experience that there are some acts of so-called freedom that destroy freedom. Offer yourselves to sin, for instance, and it's your last free act. But offer yourselves to the ways of God and the freedom never quits. All your lives you've let sin tell you what to do. But thank God you've started listening to a new master, one whose commands set you free to live openly in his freedom!

Closing Prayer

Father, thank you for freeing me! Help me to be conscious of my freedom and live every day with that knowledge. When I start to feel as if I'm in a prison, remind me that you have already paid my ransom, once and for all.

Please help these scriptures sink into my heart and soul. Let them sink deeper in, every time I read and speak them. Please guide me through this day and let the knowledge that I am free frame every thought I have and dictate every action I take. In Jesus' name. Amen.

Day 5 Exercise

If you feel like you are living in a prison that Satan has you in, don't let him keep you there! It might seem as though it's inescapable, but Jesus has already paid the price for your freedom. This doesn't always mean that it's easy to step out. Continually speak God's truth aloud and combat Satan's lies. Surround yourself with other Christians and ask them to pray for these chains to be broken once and for all.

CHAPTER 13: DAY 6 - I AM A NEW CREATION

You are continually being made new, day by day.

It might not seem like it. More likely, it seems like we're living the same day over and over. We tend to view ourselves as the "same old me" who never seems to change. We go to the *same* places and do the *same* things with the *same* people.

But is that *really* the truth? Think of yourself twenty, ten, or even just two years ago. Were you the same person then as you are now? Absolutely not. But many times, we have such a focused lens, that we don't notice the changes. Of course, many things about our character are the same. I don't deny that. But, I'm saying that you are continuously growing, whether you realize it or not.

If we accept the fact that we are continuously growing and changing, the next step is that we must be conscious of what we are feeding. What we feed, grows. So, if we continue to feed our sin nature (that is no longer part of us), we are growing in sin, and further from

God's purpose. On the other hand, if we're feeding our souls with God's truth, we will be growing in Him. Either way, we're still growing.

When we continue to feed our sin nature, we're also allowing Satan to build roadblocks that keep us from our purpose. I don't say this to lay guilt or condemnation on you (remember, there is no condemnation in Christ) instead; I say it to make you aware of Satan's schemes. He doesn't have too many moves. He doesn't have to think outside of the box because we usually fall for the classics! But, if you're aware of it, you'll know how to spot it. And never forget that God's Spirit, our helper, is always there to guide us. This includes deciphering Satan's lies and tricks.

At the moment we accept God's invitation, we are instantaneously forgiven and given His Spirit. But God also has a long-game. We are continuously being transformed over time. This is referred to as the process of sanctification. We won't be fully sanctified until we're in heaven. But God, through His Spirit who lives in us, is continually molding us into the person He wants us to be.

The fantastic news is that, as we grow in Christ, and as He continues to transform us through His Spirit, choosing God over the world will become more natural. But, it is a choice that we must make over and over. God does the heavy lifting in this work. But, we have to choose to agree with Him and also disagree with Satan and our old, dead sin nature.

Here are a few ways to do that:

Immerse Yourself in His Truth

First, immerse yourself in God's truth so that you can decipher His voice. This can only come from scripture. Yes, God does still speak to us in many ways (through other people, thoughts, dreams, visions, etc.). But, none of these will ever contradict what God says in His word. If you think that God is telling you to leave your spouse because he wants you to be with someone else, I have news for you. That is not God's voice. That is Satan or one of his minions, disguising himself as the voice of God. God will never be confusing or contradictory. John tells us: "Beloved, do not believe every spirit, but test the spirits to see whether they are from God because many false prophets have gone out into the world." 1 John 4:1(NASB) "Testing the spirits" basically means to measure it against God's word. If it contradicts it, run the other way!

Invest in Your Relationship

Second, invest in your relationship with God. Think about it, if you are in a genuinely close relationship with someone, it's not enough to only pay attention to them once every other Sunday for about an hour. Relationships require time and attention. If you're struggling in this area, I want to encourage you. Many people feel guilty for not having a "close enough" relationship with God, and so to get rid of the guilt, they simply focus on something else. It's human nature. But, instead of running from it, set some time aside every day to connect with God.

Another danger is that this can become a "to-do" list item to check off. But it doesn't have to be! To compare it to a human relationship, how would it feel if your significant other, friend, or child said: "Phew. Got those ten minutes over with! I'm done with you for the day. I can check that off my list." It wouldn't feel very loving. Again, I don't say this to lay guilt on you, but instead to open your eyes. Just like any new relationship, it might be a little weird at first. But the good news is that God already knows you inside and out, and He still loves you. There's nothing that He doesn't already know. So, tell Him, "God, I don't know how to do this! I want to get closer to you, but I don't know how. Please change my heart and mind, in Jesus' name." Of course, those are not magic words. Say it in your own words. You can talk to Him just like you talk to a friend. It will become more natural over time with practice.

Follow His Promptings

As your relationship with God grows, you will hear from Him. Simply be obedient to what He's asking you to do. We tend to overthink things. We'll ask, "God, is this *really* you?" Or if something makes no logical (otherwise known as human or worldly) sense, we tend to dismiss or overanalyze it. Many times the things that God asks us to do ***don't*** make human sense. But, if you are obedient in what He's asking you to do, He will lead you on a fantastic adventure through life - one with a purpose and worth living!

A common question would be how to know if you're actually hearing from God. Many people are hesitant to make a move unless they are 100% sure that it's from God. Although this subject is one that could fill many volumes, my suggestion is to start small. Although I don't know precisely what God is going to ask you to do, it's doubtful that He will start by asking you to quit your job and move to another country to be a missionary. Of course, He ***does*** ask people to do this, but it's usually a request to someone who strongly and regularly hears His voice. If you feel a prompting to call an old friend, compliment someone (it might even be something specific), or give a larger tip to your waitress, etc., don't overthink it. There's no need to pray for a sign and make sure it's "really from God"; just do it. Again, God knows your heart. So, even if giving a more substantial tip wasn't a direct message from Him, you're still letting Him know that your heart desires to be obedient to Him. As you practice being obedient to promptings, He will trust you with more. It's not only going to build your faith, but you will be living out one of your purposes, which is to be an ambassador of God.

Have you ever heard a word of encouragement at exactly the right time, or had someone fulfill a need for you when you needed it most? It might be a coincidence. But, more likely, it was someone being prompted by God to take action, and they were obedient. You are God's agent in the world. Listen for your next assignment and then immediately take action.

Through all of this, God is making us new every day. Even when the changes are so small that we don't notice them, it is still happening. Let's dive into some prayer and scripture meditation to help us embed this into our souls.

CHAPTER 14: DAY 6 PRAYER AND SCRIPTURE MEDITATION

Opening Prayer

God, you are not only my creator, but you are my re-creator! Every day you are gradually and lovingly molding me into the person who you want me to be.

I often listen to the messages of others, the media and the enemy instead of to you. When I listen to their voices, I attempt to mold myself into what *they* say I should be, instead of letting you have your way to shape me in the way that you desire. I'm so sorry for pushing back. I desire to be my true self, the person who you want me to be. I just need help surrendering to you. I'm so thankful that when I do surrender to you, I can fully trust that you will take care of me, because you want what's best for me. I'm so grateful that you have a perfect plan for my life.

Please help me to notice when I am trying to mold myself and then help me to recalibrate my thoughts and attention on you and what you have for me.

Please help me to truly hear and fully internalize your words. Write these scriptures on my heart and never let me forget them. Let your words give me strength to step into my true identity as your child and reject any messages that say otherwise. Remind me that you are constantly making me new so I can leave the past behind and move forward in your love. Amen.

Scripture Meditation

Read each of the following scripture passages, as well as the personalized version of each one, several times. Then say each one aloud, at least twice. Let the words wash over you. Instead of rushing through the reading, take time to internalize and own each passage.

2 Corinthians 5:17 (WEB)

Therefore if anyone is in Christ, he is a new creation. The old things have passed away. Behold, all things have become new.

Let's make this verse personal:
"Since I am in Christ, I am a new creation. The old things have passed away. Behold, all things have become new!"

2 Corinthians 4:16 (NIV)

Therefore we do not lose heart. Though outwardly we are wasting away, yet inwardly we are being renewed day by day.

Personalized version:
"I will not lose heart. Though outwardly I am wasting away, inwardly I am being renewed day by day!"

1 Peter 1:3-4 (MSG)

What a God we have! And how fortunate we are to have Him, this Father of our Master Jesus! Because Jesus was raised from the dead, we've been given a brand-new life and have everything to live for, including a future in heaven—and the future starts now!

Let's personalize the second half of that passage:
"Because Jesus was raised from the dead, I've been given a brand-new life and have everything to live for, including a future in heaven - and the future starts now!"

Isaiah 1:18 (WEB)

"Come now, and let's reason together," says Yahweh: "Though your sins are as scarlet, they shall be as white as snow. Though they are red like crimson, they shall be as wool."

God is speaking in this verse. Imagine Him speaking over you:

"Though your sins are as scarlet, they shall be as white as snow. Though they are red like crimson, they shall be as wool."

Isaiah 43:18-19 (NIV)

"Forget the former things; do not dwell on the past. See, I am doing a new thing! Now it springs up; do you not perceive it? I am making a way in the wilderness and streams in the wasteland."

Again, this is God speaking in this verse. Imagine Him speaking over you:

"Forget the former things; do not dwell on the past. See, I am doing a new thing! Now it springs up; do you not perceive it? I am making a way in the wilderness and streams in the wasteland."

Romans 6:4 (NRSV)

Therefore we have been buried with Him by baptism into death, so that, just as Christ was raised from the dead by the glory of the Father, so we too might walk in newness of life.

Personalized version:

"I have been buried with Him by baptism into death so that just as

Christ was raised from the dead by the glory of the Father, I too might walk in the newness of life!"

Revelation 21:3b-4 (NIV)

He will dwell with them. They will be his people, and God himself will be with them and be their God. 'He will wipe every tear from their eyes. There will be no more death' or mourning or crying or pain, for the old order of things has passed away.

Let's personalize the second part of that passage:

"He will wipe every tear from my eyes. There will be no more death or mourning or crying or pain, for the old order of things has passed away."

Closing Prayer

Father, thank you for not only for giving me a brand new start through Jesus, but also for continuing to make me new every day! What a privilege and honor to be shaped by you, the creator of the entire universe! Please alert me when I'm trying to fit into a worldly mold, instead of being molded and made new by you. Then help me to stay willing to be molded.

Help these words sink into my heart and soul. Let them sink deeper in, every time I hear and speak them. Please guide me through this day and let the knowledge that I have been, and continue to be made new frame every thought that I have and also dictate every action that I take. In Jesus' name. Amen.

Day 6 Exercise

Do you believe that you are continually being made new? Or do you feel like you're stuck and never changing? Spend a while with God and let Him speak directly to your heart. Ask Him to bring to mind all the ways in which you are a different person than you were two or more years ago.

If you've been trying to squeeze yourself into a worldly mold and you no longer want to feel that pressure, then tell Him that you are willing to be molded by Him and ask Him to take over from here. He can be trusted and will mold you into the very best version of you there can be!

CHAPTER 15: CONCLUSION

Thank you for reading *Who I Am in Christ*! I hope and pray that this book has been a blessing to you. Only God and His Word have the power to change you. But I hope this book has opened a door to understanding and has sparked a desire to practice living in your true identity.

To receive a **free printable pdf of flashcards** featuring all of the Bible verses covered in the scripture meditation portion of this book, please visit: **sandrajc.com/identity**. Instructions on how to download them will be delivered to your inbox!

If you've enjoyed this book, please leave me a review on the platform where you purchased or borrowed it from. I would be extremely grateful. Thank you!

May God bless you like crazy, my dear sibling in Christ! Now, get out there and live out your true identity!

Love,
Sandra

REFERENCES

Hypocrisy definition. Retrieved from
https://www.dictionary.com/browse/hypocrisy?%20s=ts

Identity definition. Retrieved from
https://www.lexico.com/en/definition/identity

After DNA test, Rockville man discovers he's an African prince
(2019, March 6). Retrieved from
https://www.wusa9.com/article/news/after-dna-test-rockville-man-
discovers-hes-an-african-prince/65-58c0638b-2762-4d13-ae0a-
be521340c149

Scripture quotations marked NIV are taken from THE HOLY
BIBLE, NEW INTERNATIONAL VERSION®, NIV® Copyright ©
1973, 1978, 1984, 2011 by Biblica, Inc.® Used by permission. All
rights reserved worldwide.

Scripture quotations marked MSG are taken from THE MESSAGE,
copyright © 1993, 2002, 2018 by Eugene H. Peterson. Used by

Made in the USA
Columbia, SC
21 December 2020